I Can Talk with My

I can talk with my hands.

You can, too.

This is my dad.
My dad can talk with his hands.

This is how I say "Dad."
Now you try it.

**My dad helps people.
He is a police officer.**

*The police officer is showing the sign for "stop."

This is how he says "police officer."
Now you try it.

This is my mom.
My mom can talk with her hands.

This is how I say "Mom."
Now you try it.

My mom helps people.
She is a doctor.

*The girl is showing the sign for "sick."
The doctor is showing the sign for "feel."

This is how she says "doctor."
Now you try it.

This is my best friend.
She can talk with her hands.

This is how we say "best friend."
Now you try it.

My best friend has a baby brother.
We talk to the baby.

This is how we say "baby."
Now you try it.

This is how we all say "I love you!"
Now you try it!